How Finance and Plan Your Real Estate Investing Business

Setting it Up Right the First Time and Getting it Right

By
Don Loyd, Ph.D.

Real Estate Investor and
Managing Real Estate Broker

How to Finance and Plan Your Real Estate Investing Business
Setting it Up Right the First Time and Getting it Right

DreamMaker Press, LLC
Denver, Colorado

ISBN-13:
978-1539939467

ISBN-10:
1539939464

Team Work Makes the Dream Work

Books by Don Loyd

Creating Wealth for Women
Creating Wealth in Declining Real Estate Markets
Creating Wealth Manual
The Cure for Declining Income
Move in Now – Buy Later
Taking Back Your Life
How to Use a Buy/Sell Analysis
I Can Be an Author
Creative Real Estate Your Way to Riches
The Right Real Estate Exit Strategy
How to Buy Your First Home
Developing Attitudes for Life Change
How to Improve Your Credit Rating
Living the Dream
A Practical Guide for the FSBO
Mortgage Magic
Retirement Recovery Guide
The Business of Real Estate Investing
The Six Figure Real Estate Broker
The Secret to 7 Figures

TABLE OF CONTENTS

About the Author – pg 5

Introduction – pg 6

Chapter 1 – pg 8
        Financing Your Business

Chapter 2 - pg 21
        Watch Out for Pitfalls

Chapter 3 – pg 27
        What is Your Exit Strategy?

Chapter 4 – pg
        Profitable Prospecting

Chapter 5 – pg 44
Selling Your Investment Property

Chapter 6 – pg 51
Plan Your Work and Work Your Plan

Chapter 7 – page 55
        Real Estate Glossary

About Don Loyd

Don Loyd, Ph.D., has been active in real estate since 1970 when he purchased his first property. Since that time, he has successfully been active as a Private Lender, Builder, Developer, Bank Loan Originator, Real Estate Broker, and more.

A Best Selling Author, his books on Personal Development, Business, Real Estate and Real Estate Investing have proven to be valuable information to a growing number of professionals.

In addition to leading Oregon Real Estate Investors Network, he serves as the Managing Principle Broker for Enetra Real Estate in Clackamas, Oregon where he teaches real estate and marketing to the Brokers working under him.

He is always looking to add quality Brokers. Please contact him if you would like to learn how Enetra may assist in your success. Email him at:
SignMeUp@DonLoyd.com.

Introduction

Become a Real Estate Investor

Real Estate Investing is an excellent way to earn income that will far surpass any "job" related income. If you do your homework on each transaction, you are almost guaranteed a solid return on your investment. You just need to research your options, create a workable plan, and check every step of the process with your own eyes. If you do these things, you greatly increase your chances of success!

It does take more effort and patience than traditional methods of investing. However, the returns are far more gratifying and potentially larger, too. Rather than just pushing a button to buy and sell, you are directly involved with every step of the process. The rewards are directly linked to the effort you place into it. Better yet, you have the potential to profit from every investment, every time.

In this book, we're going to go over everything you need to know to get started in as a Real Estate Investor. By the time you finish this book, you should be ready to start investing and creating wealth. Will you need more information that is presented here for the long haul? You bet! This book, while useful in getting started, is only the tip of the iceberg I suggest that you will become a life-long learned of this craft.

In good markets and bad, it's possible to turn a profit and help get you out of a dead end, going now where JOB (Just Over Broke).

I wish you well as you begin your journey.

The Author

Chapter 1
Financing Your Business

So you want to be a real estate investor! Good for you.

No other opportunity exists that give you as much opportunity as does real estate investing. But, how are you going to fund this new adventure? Let's talk about that:

Conventional Financing Options

Although conventional financing is an option for real estate investments, for several reasons it is typically not the first type sought. By definition, conventional financing is any loan not eligible for federal insurance or guaranteed by a government agency.

Examples of government agencies are Housing and Urban Development (HUD), Government National Mortgage Association (GNMA), Federal Housing Association (FHA),

Veterans Administration (VA), and the Farmers Home Administration (FmHA).

The various programs are required to meet the guidelines of Fannie Mae or Freddie Mac and sometimes referred to as conforming loans. The most obvious guideline limitation is the maximum loan limit Fannie Mae and Freddie Mac and adjusted each year to account for the change in average home sales prices nationwide.

Government-sponsored and monitored programs typically have a required laundry list of criteria before financing can be approved. As with most government-managed processes, securing financing for one of these programs often takes longer than conventional loans approved onlyby the bank providing the financing.

Many types of conventional loan programs are available. The programs include fixed rate, adjustable rate (ARM), balloon, biweekly, and convertible. In addition to the types of conventional loans, loan programs also offer a variety of approval criteria and features.

The terms, loan-to value, varying income, no-income-verification, and various credit score requirements, are just a few variables given different levels of consideration to achieve the desired outcome. In other words, loan officers have more to work with in conventional lending situations when seeking approval and to sell you or your business on your behalf. Real estate investment loans are not always considered conventional. As a result, you are not given the same terms as someone buying the home to reside in.

Buying investment property for rental purposes, or to renovate and sell again, is considered a commercial investment and commercial loan terms apply. Many of the residential loan approval criteria are also applicable for commercial loan approval and consideration as well.

Much like residential mortgage loans, different banks offer programs and packages for their commercial lenders. Always do your homework before you accept loan terms from any one institution. Ask about the difference between conventional residential and commercial. Ask about programs specific to your type of business. If you ask enough of the right questions, banks may then begin to offer more information than they otherwise would have.

Most loan officers are paid in a salary-plus commission structure. They want to secure financing for you, however, they may also be motivated to sell you loan programs that offer them a higher commission. So, be sure to ask enough of the right questions so they present all of the options.

Ultimately, the decision for loan approval comes from a higher power than the loan officer. The decision will come from either a local board or a corporate underwriting department. If you are working with a government involved loan program, the decision for approval comes from the sponsoring government program.

Don't give out your Social Security Number or your business identification number to every loan officer you talk with. There is truth to the fact that every time a credit check is run against your Social Security Number it pulls your credit rating down.

Creative Financing Options

"No money down," exclaimed the naysayer, "you can't do that. It's not ethical." Many people watch the "How to Buy Real Estate" infomercials on late night and weekend television and see slick productions and pitchmen promising riches beyond belief if only the viewer will use their credit card and call in.

In fairness, there is some solid information being offered (sometimes, I watch them, too). There is a lot of hype from folks who make their money selling expensive programs and boot camps. If you purchase their program, you have to have the tenacity and discipline to read the materials and follow their prescribed formula to make a go of it. But let's get to the real question:

Can you really buy real estate with no money down? The answer is, yes!

People have been led to believe it's impossible to purchase property without using your own cash. However, I've been doing it successfully since the late 1970s when I was forced to simply to survive. Much of what I know is a direct result of the real estate depression (not a slow down or recession) in Bend, Oregon, which began at that time and ran through the mid-1980s. Things were not pretty— but I learned a lot of valuable lessons during that time.

I regularly purchase with little or no cash out of my pocket. In fact, I closed a $5,500,000 real estate purchase without using my own money. In addition, I actually received a check at the end of closing. I almost never buy a house if I have to pay money out of pocket. Perhaps the more important question is: *Can you afford 100-percent financing and still enjoy cash flow?*

There are loan programs where 100-percent loans are available, but the payments are extremely high and the end result may be losing the property. I teach my protégées to ask four questions when entering into a real estate purchase:

> ➢ Does this purchase create wealth?
> ➢ How much money out of my pocket will this transaction take?
> ➢ When do I get that money back?
> ➢ Does this project have a positive cash flow?

If you have positive answers to these questions, you may have a good deal. Before you spend your hard-earned money for a dream of real estate riches, here is a list of ways to purchase with no money down.

Talk to Your Lender

One member of your success team (and you should have a team in place) should be a lender with whom you regularly do business. Call that team member and ask about zero down loan programs.

There are options available to you—especially if you are a first time homebuyer. There are also FHA and federal VA loans that are very close to zero down.

It is possible (check with your lender for availability) to get an 80-percent loan-to-value first mortgage and a 20-percent second, but be careful. The monthly payments may be too expensive to justify the purchase.

It is imperative you run an investment analysis for each property you consider for purchase. The truth is in the numbers, and your lender will be pleased to see that you get that, even before you talked to them. If you can prove through your analysis that it is a wise investment, that will go a long way to achieving success in securing a loan.

Home Equity Line of Credit -- (HELO)

One thing I do is carry a Home Equity Line of Credit (called HELOC) on each rental I own. Then if cash is needed to close a deal I can write a check from the account. At this writing, I have more than $600,000 in credit lines from my HELOC loans. One bank has given me a credit card tied to my HELOC with a credit line of $99,999.

You should, however, use caution when using the line of credit. The first thing I ask myself before drawing money from a HELOC is, when will I get this money back to pay off the loan? If you can't answer that question, do not borrow the money. Any cash advance will increase your monthly payments.

Also make sure you are not upside down with your cash flow. That is a common mistake of many new investors. The financial analysis you prepare before you purchase a property shouldn't be sweetened in any way to make the deal look better on paper than it really is. If you can't achieve cash flow or a reasonable return on your investment, find a different property.

Seller Financing

Don't overlook the possibility of the seller lending you the down payment. If you are marketing and talking to the right sellers – specifically motivated ones, they may well help you get your first mortgage by loaning you enough money to close the deal.

I frequently use that technique. I have had a seller loan me as much as $500,000 with no interest for the first 6 months. I then made sure I turned the property over before 6 months.

By the way, the $500,000 could just as easily be $1,000,000 on the right deal. If the seller has a lot of equity or is in foreclosure, creative options are available.

Raise the Price and Lower the Terms

If you offer the seller more than he is asking, you may be able to pull this one off. He has to be willing to accept the down payment in the form of a note if the house appraises well enough to justify the price increase.

For example, a seller is asking $250,000 for his house with a $15,000 down payment and he is willing to carry the balance of $235,000. You offer him $255,000, or gets a little more return for the extra risk involved. Use your imagination. That's the only thing that restricts your success.

Use Your Investment Property Inventory

On occasion, I borrowed against another property I own. I currently have a note and trust deed on an investment property that I used instead of cash. That meant I didn't have to come up with dollars to close the deal and gives me tremendous flexibility. Imagine what is possible if you don't always have to borrow the money for your down payment.

Find an Investor

One trick I teach my protégées is to search for successful people who want to be real estate investors but do not have the time to spend on research. They have the cash and financial strength to do a deal so you help out by supplying the time it takes to locate and negotiate the purchase.

I have several protégées who are in a position to make $100,000 to $500,000 each year without using their cash or credit. They will not do a deal unless there is at least $30,000 to $35,000 total profit in the transaction. Their share in that size of profit is $15,000 (for a $30,000 profit). This is a great way to get started as an investor. You provide the work and expertise and let your partner supply the money and credit.

Use Your Commission

If you are a real estate broker/agent, use your commission to get what you want. I use mine when I purchase real estate such as single-family homes, duplexes, bare land, or subdivisions. On one transaction alone I made $350,000. The seller told me what price he wanted, and I added my commission to it – and the property appraised properly.

On single-family homes, using your own commission works well when you are dealing with a For Sale by Owner (FSBO). After we agree to a sales price, I have added a fee of 3 percent for closing costs paid by the seller and 7 percent for a sales commission I then used on the down payment. Again, be creative. As long as everything is fully disclosed and the house appraises appropriately, it will work.

Lease Option

If you have never done a lease option, also called to a Rent-To-Own, you owe it to yourself to start. There are several great reasons to lease option. Some argue that it's best to control rather than own. This is especially true if you have poor credit and you can't, or won't, find a financial partner.

You can negotiate leases with landlords who are tired of dealing with rentals or an owner and who can't sell a house. Negotiate a small down payment ($100? in the form of "option consideration") but be sure that the payment, or a portion of it, is deducted from the sales price.

You should maintain the right to sublease. If possible, make sure your monthly payment is below current rents, then offer to sell the property on a lease option at a higher price than you negotiated, with $5,000 down in the form of option consideration.

Then charge an extra $100 to $200 per month in order for you to realize positive cash flow. For a complete strategy, see my book on lease-options

Trade for It

Another technique is to offer the seller something they might need or want. Cash is not the only form of payment. I have traded many times for down payments.

Possibilities include such things as boats, cars, recreational vehicles, tractors, gemstones, silver or gold, or personal services (I have done all of these while buying and selling). Discover what the seller really wants and offer it for trade.

One of my mentors, Barney Zick (now diseased), has a tremendous course on the subject of negotiations. See if you can find his course. It will be well worth whatever you have to pay for it. All of his product are worthy of you reviewing. Check out http://www.realestatecoursesandbooks.com/barney-zick/

Your Family and Friends

You may be able to borrow the money you need from your family, friends, or business partner, but I urge you to be fair and honest with them. Many friendships and family relationships have been strained or lost because of a bad business deal. You may want to offer them a portion of the profit when the property is sold. If they are willing to loan you money, nurture the relationship so you will have the opportunity to borrow again if needed.

If you learn to invest in real estate without using your own hard-earned cash, you will realize returns that can exceed 1,000 percent at a time when many think a 10 percent or 50 percent return is good. If you have money in the bank, I have a challenge for you; on your next real estate transaction, think outside the box and do not use any of your own money. It will open up a whole new world for you.

Your Credit Rating

I now want to turn your attention to credit. There are many real estate gurus who tell us we don't need good credit to make millions of dollars in the real estate market. While that is certainly true, and I have shown many investors how that can be done, with good credit you can make much more.

Poor credit is a weight around your neck that can kill many good deals. It limits your alternatives and options when the money market dries up. Besides, it is a reflection of your character. A person who isn't faithful paying their monthly bills is a person whose word is not very believable.

The person with "challenged" credit, as we sometimes generously say, has a flashing neon sign on his back that declares: "I know I promised to pay, and I had good intentions, but I decided to buy a new car and take my wife to dinner instead."

Here is what I suggest:

> **1. Run a credit report** and make a list of your debts. This will identify who you have to pay and when you should pay.

2. Don't roll your debt into a credit card and then another. While this may seem like the answer to your problem, you are only creating a larger monster to deal with later.

3. Prioritize your credit list. When facing our financial problems, my wife and I had to work hard to get back to square one. We took the following:

> a. We listed our creditors and chose to pay off the ones with the least amount of balance while making minimum payments to the others.

> b. When the first debt was paid off, we took the amount we were paying and applied it to the next one on the list.

> c. We repeated the process until we were paying large amounts each month to the final credit card.

> d. We changed our lifestyle. We rarely ate out; we drove used cars and took low-cost family vacations only if we could do it without using our credit card. My wife shopped for bargains and clipped vendor coupons. It was difficult but well worth it to get back on our feet.

4. Use credit cards sparingly, keep low balances and pay on time. Some writers advise us to destroy our credit cards once they are paid in full. I think it's better to keep them and use them carefully to show the credit reporting agencies that you use credit wisely. In that way you can rebuild your credit rating, making available more options to fund your real estate purchases.

5. Establish a realistic monthly budget and stick to it. It's the only way to get out of debt and rehabilitate your credit.

6. Be extremely careful with the equity in your home. You don't want to draw out your equity and pay off your debt if you have not cured the problem. I've seen many people get into debt, refinance their home (or get a Home Equity Line of Credit), and spend their equity while not addressing the real issue of uncontrollable spending.

7. There are many resources available to help you overcome your indebtedness so use them. It has been said, "The more you learn, the more you earn." That is true with regard to building a good credit rating.
Use these basic steps to start immediately paying down your debts. You will have many more nights of sound sleep knowing that the phone is not going to ring with a collector at the other end wanting his money. As a bonus, you will be able to get more real estate under contract, and closed, as more avenues of finance open for you based on a strong credit rating.

Chapter 2
Watch Out for Pitfalls

With a slowing real estate market, some real estate investors try to survive financially by refinancing their investment properties, hoping to generate enough cash to keep their heads above water. While that approach may simply serve as a bandage, unless the underlying problem is addressed, the short-term solution could lead to a financially devastating crisis.

There is a widely held real estate investment doctrine that suggests the best way to purchase real estate is maximize the loan amount (over finance it) to get the transaction closed and move on. That is advocated for two reasons. First, it allows for a zero-down approach to investing and second, it can generate cash.

While I believe those two reasons may be valid, they are only insofar as the transaction merits it. The approach works if you are buying significantly below the current market value or if appreciation is rocketing into the stratosphere. In the case of the latter, you should be warned that at some point the rocket always runs out of fuel and crashes back on earth. Take care the rocket doesn't hit you on its downward plummet.

Smart real estate investors resist the temptation to over finance property simply for the sake of

generating cash. They have at least three reasons for this.

Reason #1

It's best not to over finance your property because you pay a premium if you exceed 80 percent of the value to the loan amount. Historically, lenders embraced the notion that if their investment (loan) is at that value, or less, th risk is acceptable. If the loan value is more than 80 percent, the loan gets more risky for the lender. That is why PMI (Private Mortgage Insurance) exists. PMI ensures that in the event of a default, the lender will not be liable for a loss in excess of 80 percent.

There is another way to accomplish the same thing. You can get a second mortgage (a note and Deed of Trust) on the property for the amount needed above 80 percent. The interest rate will be higher than the first mortgage, and in some cases much higher, but at least it is tax deductible.

There have been some recent proposed changes to the tax deductibility of PMI. Be sure to talk to your mortgage broker before you make a final decision on whether to secure a second mortgage or use PMI.

Then, of course, there are now 100-percent loans available. But before you go out and get one, be forewarned—the payment will eat you alive. The high interest rate charged for a 100-percent loan makes the transaction fundamentally undoable if you are paying retail.

If you are considering that option, check and double check the property analysis you will perform to ensure you are making a wise decision. The bottom line is: the higher percentage of loan amount you borrow, the more you pay for the privilege of borrowing. There is a balancing act here and it will behoove you to learn everything you can about the pros and cons of all of the available financing options.

Reason #2

If you over finance your property, you can't consistently enjoy positive cash flow. For the real estate investor, cash flow is the name of the game. If you compromise by thinking that you will have only an extra $200 to pay out of my pocket each month, you will soon be out of business. If you do that 10 times, you have to come up with $2,000 each month simply to say you're a real estate investor. How smart is that?

I received a call from a friend who has several properties with a negative cash flow. The payments are eating him alive. The call was a request that I take over his payments on one of his properties and he would deed me the house. I couldn't do it because the rent was several hundred dollars less than the payment and I couldn't see a quick exit strategy.

If you don't have positive cash flow (or equity), your options are limited. In addition, your dream of leaving your current job to become a full-time real estate investor is put on hold while you figure a way out of your mess. Those who have gotten themselves into this mess in the first place did so because they either didn't do the math, or didn't do the math correctly.

Reason #3

If your property is over financed, you will have a difficult time getting rid of it if the need arises. My advice is to make sure you can dump the property easily before you close the purchase transaction.

Another true story: I received calls from two separate investors who had property they had to unload. Fortunately for them, they could do it. Their loan to value was about 80 percent with no cash out of pocket when they bought. Both investors sold to me. As a result of more experience and networking structure, I was able to resell the two houses in less than 48 hours.

This was possible in our slowing market because my sellers were into the property without being over financed. I was also able to give my buyers a great deal with great terms that promised positive cash flow. If your exit strategy does not include a winning situation for your end buyer, you do not have an effective strategy. Use this as a general rule: every transaction has to be a win-win for both parties. If it is not, then you shouldn't buy it.

Financing has its place. I seldom use any of my own money to close a deal. When I do use my money, I know when I'm getting it back. I'm not suggesting that 100- percent financing is wrong for the real estate investor. I'm saying that 100-percent financing is wrong in most cases if you are paying retail.

Any time you find real estate in which to invest at 80 percent of value or less, by all means find a loan for the entire amount if your exit strategy fits the loan. You will have succeeded in creating wealth and probably positive cash flow.

Whenever that is possible, take the leap forward.

Financing can be a two-edged sword. Over finance and you can find yourself choking to death. Used properly, financing can create wealth to help you realize financial independence, plan for the future, and provide you with the ability to give generously to a worthy cause.

What is Creating Wealth and What is Cash Flow?

Too often beginning real estate investors confuse cash flow with wealth building. It's true that cash flow is essential to filling your wealth bucket; however, you can be building wealth in other ways that do not necessarily rely on cash flow. An example of that would be a long-term rental property. If the rent you collect puts you in a positive cash flow situation (and that could mean only $25 a year), you are still building wealth. Every rent payment that tenant makes, which you in turn apply to the mortgage on the property, is money that is building your wealth.

As long as you keep that property properly maintained, and are careful about who you select as tenants for your long-term rental investments, you should also be experiencing appreciation on that property over time in addition to the equity you are gaining from paying down the mortgage against it.

Long-term rentals are just one possible real estate investment opportunity and the pros and cons of that option are worthy of having a book written specifically on that topic. Many have.

The common denominator between this wealth building scenario and others that I have already provided is that the end result is that you had a working strategy to buy, make money, then if you choose, to get out and take that money to invest in a bigger and better opportunity.

"Cash flow" is a generic term that can be used differently depending on the context in which it is used. We are using the term cash flow to mean spendable dollars generated after expenses are paid. Cash flow is most commonly used in real estate investing to evaluate the performance of a particular project or your entire business as a whole.

Creating wealth or wealth building is the dollars that you have earned and can add to your asset portfolio in either dollars or capital. Each time that tenant makes a rent payment on that long-term rental, you have just earned more capital that you can leverage for spendable dollars or sell for spendable dollars.

The amount of money in your checking account does not define your total net worth. If you are doing it right, however, you will have significant cash flow and continue building wealth through capital investments simultaneously.

Chapter 3
What is Your Exit Strategy?

As a leader of a growing real estate investment club I'm often asked, how do you find good deals? I had a new protégé demand, "Why should I go out and look at the property? You're supposed to find me a good deal." She failed to understand that if I found a "good deal," I would buy it!

First, let's define what constitutes a "good deal." To you, that may seem obvious, but if you can't clearly define what it means to you, how do you know when you've found one? Consider the following factors when defining what a good deal means to you.

What is your exit strategy?

One factor and perhaps the first to consider is your exit strategy. What are you going to do with a specific property? Is the strategy to hold, flip, lease option, wholesale, fix and flip, or?

Before I close a transaction, I know what I'm going to do with the property. Sometimes my strategy changes, but for the most part it pretty much remains the same. If I find a duplex in my home town that I can pick up for 60 percent of value I will clean it up, hold it long term (more than 12 months), and then sell it.

If the duplex happens to be in Klamath Falls, Oregon, which is about a 6 -hour drive south from where I live, I will likely sell it with great owner terms for a small profit and move it quickly. I will take that approach because I don't want to manage property that far away.

What are your goals?

Each of us has goals unique to us. I teach my protégés to write a life purpose statement and build goals around that. Once you understand your purpose, you are in a much better position to define your goals and develop a plan to achieve those goals.

If your goal is to create passive positive cash flow of $10,000 each month so you can live on $5,000 and give away $5,000 to philanthropic projects, then you need to manage your activity and focus on your objectives in a way that will enhance your ability to achieve the overall goal.

Let's suppose then, that an opportunity comes along that would take you in a different direction. Although it's a great opportunity, it might not be in your best interest if not aligned with your life purpose.

What are your skills?

If you don't know the difference between a power drill and a chain saw, you had better stay away from houses and apartment units that need to be repaired before you rent them. Unless you are looking at a property with an eye toward learning something new, stay clear of properties that require skills you are unable or unwilling to provide. The investment opportunity may not be as good at it appears.

What is your financial strength?

This one is a biggie. I've seen new real estate investors get deep into debt and unable to complete transactions because they tried to purchase a good deal, only to lose it and other property as well.

For example, unless you have deep pockets, you may want to stay away from vacant land. Investing in vacant land and building lots is a rich person's market— unless you are building houses as a strategy. There is generally no inward cash flow to help offset the flow of cash out. The good deal suddenly goes sour when you run out of money and lose all you invested in the good deal.

If you have limited resources, try to keep your investment purchases to single family homes at the lower end of the real estate investment spectrum—or a step above. Many more retail buyers and tenants are at this level, which means you have a greater chance of selling the house or filling a vacancy and ultimately realize a positive stream of income.

I know several people who got in trouble when they found a great deal. They borrowed to the hilt and made payments on empty houses. That strategy will set you up for financial disaster. It matters little that you picked up a $900,000 house for $700,000 if you cannot find a buyer or make the payments for an extended period of time. The deal may be good for someone, but is it a good deal for you?

As you can see, the term good deal is relative. Lots of good deals may be out there, but be sure the deal is good for you. This segment is a reiteration, in a different way, of the segment that tells you that you have to run the numbers.

I've said it before and I'll say it again. If it doesn't make sense on paper, then it doesn't make sense. You are, after all, investing. Risk is involved; however, you can minimize that risk dramatically by asking the right questions, doing an analysis, and acting accordingly.

Your Marketing Plan

One of the most important sections of your business plan is your marketing plan. This section is where you include a definitive description of your customers, market size, demographics, characteristics, growth prospects, trends, and sales potential.

The marketing plan is a document that outlines your strategies and describes how those strategies can directly influence the growth of your business. In the plan, you should also include plans for your future growth. A snapshot of a 3-to-5 year outcome demonstrates not only your commitment to your business but your ability to plan for the future.

A marketing plan outlines specific actions you intend to carry out necessary to attract the client or customer base that you will need to make your business successful. I once had a marketing professor who used the phrase, "You can't operate in a bubble and think you are going to be successful outside that bubble." Everything you present to the market "outside the bubble" needs to be captured in a comprehensive marketing plan. The marketing plan is the road map to the next phase of your business through captured clients and awareness of the services you are providing in your business.

Often you will find that marketing plans are a part of an overall business plan. In a real estate investment business where marketing your services to the general public may not be your first method of tapping into new business, the inclusion of the marketing plan into the business plan is still required. Going through the exercise of completing a plan is important and you should not only answer the questions necessary to complete it but ask yourself what the answers to the questions should be a year or two after you are out of the introductory phase of your business.

Tapping into the general public, versus just using networking, to secure future transactions is a viable method of achieving your goals. A marketing plan outlines the specific actions you intend to carry out to attract the attention of that future business. How would you do that?

Not only do you want to demonstrate to lenders that you have the ability to plan for future business, but you want to plant those strategies in the back of your mind so that if an opportunity that fits that strategy presents itself, you won't make the mistake of overlooking what could have been a milestone in the success of your business.

If you are eager for customers to be contacting you instead of your having to find every one of them, you may want to give this some serious thought early on, not later.

Remember, however, marketing costs money. I have seen new business owners go under because their marketing budget wasn't properly in line with their sales. Plan big, budget small, and be creative.

Marketing Plan

Research: An overview of your market.

- What is the total size of your market or markets?
- What companies within your industry have succeeded and how?

Customers: Who are your customers?

- What are their values, attitudes, and beliefs?
- Are they local, regional, national, or international?
- Are they liberal or conservative?
- Are they rich or financially challenged?
- Can you envision your client?
- Will you target other consumers, other businesses or the government?

Competition: Who is your competition?

- Do your competitors have Web sites? If yes, list the domain names. Make a list of what you like and don't like about their sites.

- What are your competitor's strengths?
- What are your competitor's weaknesses?

Your Company Strengths: What gives you the confidence that you will succeed?

- What unique benefits does your product, service, or cause provide?
- How have you branded your company so you will be remembered? Think positioning slogans such as, "Let your fingers do the walking" or "Finger lickin' good." Are market indicators in your favor?
- Do you have a top-notch management team?
- Are market demographics definitely in your favor?

Your Company Weaknesses

- Are you underfinanced?
- Do you lack technological know-how?
- Can you find all the right people for the jobs if you are outrageously successful?
- Do you have an adequate facility?
- Do you have ready access to your goods supplies or suppliers?
- Do you foresee any intellectual property problems?

Online Web site Promotion

- How do you plan to promote your site? Give a detailed listing of each effort along with its timeline
- Are you going to use "pay per click" Search Engines?
- Are you going to hire a Search Engine Marketing company?

• Do you have an online public relations plan?
Are you going to conduct an on-going linking effort?
• Do you plan to have weekly, bi-weekly, or monthly specials?
• Are you going to do anything promotional?
• Are you planning ongoing email campaigns?

Off-line Promotions

• Newspaper, magazine, radio, or television advertising campaign?
• Public relations campaign?
• Catalog, brochure, or direct mailings?

Budget
• Have you set a budget for your marketing?
• If yes, how far out did you plan the expenditures?
• How much will you outsource? If so, who will you use?
• How do you plan to generate the money to fuel your ongoing efforts?

Chapter 4
Profitable Prospecting

Prospecting will be your key to financial success. You will not be able to wake up one morning, declare yourself a real estate investor, clip your phone to your purse, and think that it will ring. Prospecting doesn't mean that you have to go knocking door to door as if you were selling cosmetics out of a briefcase.

Finding real estate investment properties can be done in many ways. That is the luxury of becoming a real estate investor, you have some freedom to work your own magic your own way, and sometimes without even getting out of your pajamas.

I am not going to feed you some line about how you can get rich quick working from home and how the world is at your fingertips from your side of the computer. But, you will be able to find some opportunities online if you look in the right places.

We have established that using the Internet is one way of uncovering opportunities to explore. Let's go over some others: tell people about your new adventure. I have been in the real estate business a long time and it has been said that everyone knows someone who is about to make a real estate change. Tell people what kind of investments you are interested in and ask them to keep an eye out and an ear open for anything that fits the criteria.

Tell them there is a Starbucks gift card in it for them if they send the information your way. When they do, be sure to follow through and send them a gift card. It's the best few dollars you will spend that week, because I assure you, another lead will follow shortly thereafter.

If you've been feeling a little cooped up but want to stick to your objectives, get in your car and drive around looking for For Sale by Owner signs. Not all For Sale by Owner properties keep ads in the paper regularly. They forget to renew with the paper or they don't want to continue to pay the costs for continued advertising. Take down the contact information on the sign and call them or even stop by if that's more your style. Find out what their objectives are and if they are willing to work with an investor to achieve their objectives in a timelier manner. Buy cheap, sell cheap, and profit.

Another possible source is identifying homes already vacant. Call them first (a normal source of information is the county clerk or a customer service representative at your favorite title company). It is pretty clear that they have already moved on and likely consider their old home a monkey on their back. Call them and find out what they would consider selling it for. Even if they're not ready to sell wholesale today, they might be ready after a few more double mortgage payments. Keep a watch for these properties and call them again in a few months if the sign is still there.

Another possible opportunity is contacting landlords with For Rent ads in the paper. If the same ad has shown up week after week, then it's possible that the landlord is ready to call it quits.

Of course, if the owner is unable to find a renter, perhaps there is good reason, and you will need to do a little research and figure out why before you write an offer. However, it might be something that you have the resources to deal with and still make a profit. Whichever it turns out to be, it is worth looking into.

Take this next suggestion seriously! Take lenders to lunch! Make a list of lenders in your area. Lenders are a superb way of finding foreclosures before they are listed with agents or put up for auction. If you can put the deal together before they accrue additional costs, it may be savings they are willing to put in your pocket. Additionally, they are in touch with clients who have property they want or need to move.

While you're meeting with these lenders you can informally interview them and find out what their area of expertise is s well as evaluate if they are someone that could or should become a key player in your team of resources.

Ask them if they know of any attorneys or accountants who specialize in real estate that would complement your team. You can also ask them about local appraisers and inspectors. Lenders are in a unique position because they come in contact with a variety of the levels of investing. Treat them to lunch and go prepared to do more than simply socialize.

Another great place to become familiar with is the courthouse. Many things such as evictions and foreclosures are required to be recorded with the county. When something is recorded with the county, it becomes public record. If it's public record, you can get to it.

Take some time to visit your county courthouse and ask questions. Find out what is recorded and where and how you can get it. Find out how frequently it would be beneficial for you to stop and check for updates. Are they recorded weekly or monthly?

A fairly obvious suggestion is to put an ad on Craigslist. That ad should be very brief and should encourage anyone who would like to sell quickly, for any reason, to call you. Indicate that you are in the business of making real estate sales happen.

Government-owned real estate can be good bargains. Most investors have heard of Housing and Urban Development (HUD) homes and Veterans Affairs (VA) homes. Those homes are foreclosed homes that the government has taken back. They usually need a good cleaning, carpet, and paint.

I know investors who buy only HUD homes and have done well. Many of these homes can be located online. There is typically a little red tape involved to make offers on government-owned properties, but once you learn the process, it will forever be a valid way of uncovering opportunities.

If a large business recently closed or laid off workers in your area, there may be several families who were living pay check to pay check that need to unload their houses quickly to keep their credit ratings in tact or prevent foreclosure.

Don't prey on the weak; rather give them an option to stay where they are, with their dignity intact while paying you rent instead of the bank a mortgage payment and provide them the option to buy back in when they can. A good investor is always looking for the win-win!

Don't Overlook the Details

You are a new real estate investor. You've found a good investment buy. What do you do? You make an offer to purchase. All states require that an offer to purchase real estate must be in writing to be enforceable. How do you do that?

The sales contract, sometimes called a purchase agreement, doesn't have to be a preprinted form (unless you are a Realtor ®) or have any special look to it. It should, however, include several pieces of information that have an impact on the sale. Here are the key pieces of information that most sales contracts will include:

1. A legal and physical description of the property being purchased. The legal description is used by the county government to identify the property even if the street address changes. The legal description of the property will never change.

2. The selling price and method of payment should be included. In most cases, a mortgage or a note and trust deed is the method of payment. I advise you to include details about the amount of the down payment, loan, and earnest money deposit. If you have any contingencies regarding loan qualification for the loan, they should be listed as well.

3. If you are the buyer, you will want to name a title and escrow company that will hold your earnest money and close the transaction.

4. You should also include in your offer the proposed date of closing. If you think there is a possibility of not meeting that date, be sure to include a provision that states the closing date may be extended an additional number of days, if needed to complete the paper work. If you do this you'll not have to write an addendum later to extend the date and it may save the deal for you. For example, if you do not meet the closing date the seller can call off the sale. I've had this happen on a few occasions.

5. What's included and what's not included in thesale should be detailed. If the seller agrees to throw in appliances or a riding lawn mower (it never hurts to ask), those items must be listed in the sales contract. Otherwise, you could end up purchasing your own appliances after closing.

6. Any warranties included with the home should be detailed in the sales contract. A description of the warranty should also be listed.

7. If the property has a well and septic, be sure to define who will pay for the water purity testing, water flow test, and septic inspection and pumping.

8. A termite and pest inspection should be conducted. The sales contract should detail not only who will pay for the inspection, but also the party responsible for any repairs if infestation or damage is discovered.

9. The exact date that the buyer will take possession of the home should be included. That date can be any time before, at, or after closing. I would include a provision that sets a set amount of rent the seller agrees to pay if he is not out of the house at the agreed date. I usually make the amount equal to my monthly payment.

10. The sales contract should include the amount of time that the seller has to respond to the offer, regardless of accepting or countering the offer. If you don't set a date of offer expiration, the seller could hold your offer for a month before responding. I usually give the seller 1 day to think over my offer.

11. Provision for arbitration or mediation is sometimes included. People do lie and deceive. And sometimes people are simply a big pain to deal with. If you include such a provision, you will likely avoid civil court action. The provision could save you thousands of dollars.

12. Either the seller or the buyer will have to pay for property insurance until the closing date. The sales contract should stipulate the responsible party.

13. Any property disclosures pertaining to the house should also be included in the sales contract. In Oregon, if the seller does not give you a property disclosure, you can withdraw your offer anytime up to, and including, the closing date. If you are the seller, be sure you give your buyer a property disclosure statement.

14. Any special provision should also be included.

15. If Mr. and Mrs. Smith are the sellers, be sure to have both sign the sales agreement. Here's a rule of thumb I use: It takes one to buy, but two to sell. You could get the closing with Mr. Smith's signature and Mrs. Smith decides she doesn't want to move. So now you're stuck. You can't take title unless both are willing to sell to you.

If I'm the buyer I want to have a purchase agreement with me when I look at a house. I may want to make an offer to purchase on that day. I may also submit the offer before I see the house. No rule exists indicating you must. Why not fax or e-mail the offer to the seller and wait to see if you have a transaction before you waste your time on a property you won't have under contract?

You can find forms you might need at Office Depot, Staples, or you can do a Google search and find online sources. Just be sure that your offer is clear and understandable and you have the seller in agreement with your offer.

Chapter 5
Selling Your Investment Property

You have purchased an investment property and now it's time to sell it. Do you use a Realtor® or go it alone? For the sake of full discloser, I am a licensed Real Estate Broker. As such, I have a certain bias.

Having stated that, one of the most challenging aspects of selling your house without using a Realtor® is putting the correct price on the house. That's the reality. If a house is overpriced, even by a few thousand dollars, the house may sit on the property for a long time. Some new investors think, "I can always come down in price, so I will price it high so I'll have negotiating room." That approach, while often used, is not well founded.

When your "For Sale by Owner" home has been sitting on the market for months without a satisfactory offer, one of the first things you wonder is if your price is too high. It may very well be. The house is not actually worth what the lender appraises. Nor is it worth the list price of the house across the street. It is worth only what someone is willing to pay.

Realtors® make it their career to understand the concepts of buying and selling homes. Selling a home requires an in-depth marketing plan that should include various forms of print, Internet, and even other forms of media advertising. Agents know when to hold open houses, how to price a, when to reduce it, and when to reduce it again, if necessary.

Look at the Facts

Having made those statements, here is what I want you to do: Think about how many qualified buyers you have shown your house to. How many of them have made offers on your home? If buyers have been coming to showings but have not been making offers, or if no one is coming to your open house presentations, the problem could very well be that your home is overpriced. It may also be that a potential buyer has some specific objection.

However, because they are working directly with the seller—you—they do not want to voice that objection. If potential buyers do not voice that objection, then you cannot address the objection.

Realtors® are middlemen for a reason. Their feelings don't get hurt when somebody says they don't like this or that. They collect the information and present it to a seller. Sometimes, if the seller addresses all of their objections, they may have a buyer willing to write an offer.

The longer your house stays on the market, the less attractive it will be to buyers. Suspicion arises when a home has been on the market for more than a couple of months, even if the price is the only thing wrong.

But there is another important consideration. Others will use your overpriced house against you to sell their house. They will do it like this: "The investor down the street is asking $275,000 for that house. I have the same size house with a larger lot and I'm only asking $260,000. Mr. Buyer, you will save $15,000 and have a larger yard— if you buy mine."

A Realtor® already knows all of this. They live and breathe it every day. They make the right decisions so you are not put into compromising situations. They know the pulse of the market, the average days on the market, who and where the competition is, and they network with the several hundred (or thousands) of other Realtors® in the city.

It is fallacy that you can save money by not using a Realtor®. If you take into consideration the advertising costs, the time for open houses, the time for all of the showings, and the time it took to put all of the sales materials together, you will realize they are actually underpaid by the time they split it with the other agent and their broker. In addition to that, how much are you worth an hour?

If you can make $10,000 a month flipping properties with the help of a Realtor® but only $5,000 a month flipping properties without the help of a Realtor® because you are spending so much time behind the desk or in your car running to showings, then the solution is clear.

There are several layers to real estate investing, and you are not going to be able to do all of them yourself. You shouldn't even try because you will fail, and then your business will fail for the wrong reasons. Delegate anything and everything that you can as long as you have competent people to delegate to and you continue to keep your finger on the pulse of the macro picture.

The best part about Realtors® is they don't get paid until you get paid. If you see an attorney or an accountant, the clock starts ticking the minute you walk into their office. With the Realtor® you pay nothing until the time of sale. Why on earth wouldn't you take advantage of that?

Do Some Research

Even when you do delegate the sales aspect of your investment properties to a Realtor®, you are still going to want to understand the language that they speak and to know enough to ask the right questions. Pay attention to what's going on in the real estate market around you. Are there more listings in your area than there were last year?

If so, you will have to be a little more competitive in pricing your home. Take some time to visit open houses of similar homes for sale in your area. Compare them to yours. Take note of the negative and positive aspects and use them to gauge your home price. In the book *The Art of War* written by Sun Tzu, a Chinese General from the 14th century, he explains that if you want to succeed you always need to know your enemy better than they know yourself. That theory applies everywhere.

Look at your property and selling price objectively. If you were in the market to purchase a new home, would you pay your asking price? By asking yourself this question, you might easily come up with an answer about cutting your asking price. Don't let your sentiments or emotions cloud your judgment. Consider your home from the point of view of someone who has no emotional attachment to the home. This is a skill that requires practice but it is essential to being successful.

Buyer Incentives

If you need to retain the asking price of your home, you might want to offer other incentives to get the attention of the buyer. Offer to pay part of the closing costs. Some lenders have a maximum amount that the seller is allowed to contribute. If your budget allows, max out your contribution to the closing costs. This will decrease the amount of cash the buyer has to spend and make the deal look more attractive.

Talk to your lender to see what can be done with incentives. Lender underwriting guidelines are always changing. Be creative and ask questions such as: How much of the down payment can I loan or gift to a buyer? Can I offer to make part of the buyer's payments for a few months? Be sure you have up-to-date information.

If after careful analysis you decide to reduce the price on your home, your Realtor® will advertise the new price. He or she will call any buyers that previously expressed an interest and let them know about the lower price. You might find that buyers are a little more eager to jump on the deal at the lowered price.

Pricing your house correctly could be the most important part of a successful sale. Rely on the expertise of your Realtor® to provide the accurate information. Successful real estate investors have found that the correct pricing of their property is the key to real estate riches.

Instead of pricing your house so that you have "dickering room," price it to sell so you can move on to the next project. Time is very important. Each day spent holding on to an overpriced house is a day lost in finding a new investment opportunity and incurred holding costs on the one you still have, and those holding costs are eating away your profits each day. Don't attempt to justify your reasons for holding on to the property.

If you are a real estate investor you, will likely find yourself taking on the role of real estate agent on occasion. When you do, you must cover all bases adequately. To get top dollar for your property, your home should be in excellent condition and ready to be shown to potential buyers. Preparing the house to show is not difficult, but to ensure success it does require proper planning and a little bit of work on your part. If you aren't going to use the services of a Realtor®, then you had better be able to see through their eyes, and what that really means is seeing through the eyes of the buyer.

Outside

First impressions are lasting ones. The outside of your home is the first thing potential buyers will see so make it clean and attractive. "Curb appeal" is what attracts potential buyers. Spruce up the outside to lure potential buyers inside. In an established neighborhood, I try to offer a neatly manicured lawn. Manicured lawns implicitly signify a well-maintained home. Make a habit of cutting your lawn weekly while the home is for sale. Consider hiring a landscape service. You can save tremendous time and effort as well as keep it looking topnotch.

Be sure to rake leaves and to sweep the sidewalks on the weekends when your house is to be shown. If you have shrubs and trees, remove debris and dead limbs to make the yard more presentable. Planting extra flowers for color or setting out potted flowers also enhances a buyer's first impression of your home.

If there is a fence, make sure it is in good shape. Consider doing repair work, if necessary, and touch it up with stain or paint. Put away lawn equipment, children's toys, and any other outdoor items. Potential buyers want to see clean and green. If you have large pets, take them to the neighbors, if possible, so they don't interfere with the showing of your for property.

Inside

The inside of your home is next on the list. People generally buy homes that appear spacious, clean, and solid. Dark colors and clutter turn off most buyers. Store everything you can live without.

If you paint your interior, use an off-white or eggshell-colored paint. You should also replace your light bulbs with brighter, higher wattage bulbs. Again, the look you are going for is bright and spacious. Clean everything thoroughly, including having carpets shampooed.

Remove as many personal items as possible. The pictures on your refrigerator door are important to you— not your potential buyer. Buyers want to visualize *their* personal items in the house, not yours—so help them.

Besides, the more personal items you remove or pack away, the more spacious and clean the home will look. Clean the oven and all appliances and be sure to polish any chrome fixtures. Be especially particular about ridding your home of any odors. Fix loose doorknobs, repair broken windowpanes or leaky windowsills. Be sure all light fixtures are secure and in good repair. Also, be sure to repair leaky pipes and reapply caulk as needed. Consider hiring a cleaning service. They can make a remarkable difference in the overall appearance of your home.

Home Inspection

Most people have a home inspection before they buy. You might want to head off a possible problem by hiring your own home inspector. He will give you a list of repairs that need to be made before selling the house. Use your judgment regarding his findings and repair anything that is a safety or functional issue.

Use the report to show potential buyers that you had the home inspected and you had the deficiencies repaired. Most buyers will accept your inspection report and not order their own. That fact is to your favor and may save you money in the long run.

The general tips I present here will get you started on preparing your home for showing. When finished, go through your home with an especially critical eye, trying to view the home from a buyer's perspective. It might also help to have a friend or neighbor to do a walkthrough of the home and critique your efforts. This will ensure a complete and thorough preparation that should boost the appeal of your home and make for a successful sale.

Chapter 6
Plan Your Work and Work Your Plan

In the real estate investment club I lead, most of the members are relatively new to real estate investing. Until recently, they could purchase anything locally and be assured of a quick profit. They could make bad choices and still look good. Some of those same people are now feeling the pinch of reality as the local market slows to a more normal rate.

Having been in robust markets that have cooled to a recession level (a recession being when *they* lose money, a depression being when *I* do), I know professional real estate investors can do certain things to prosper in any market. Here are my steps:

Have a Plan

The first step is to have a plan. If you don't have a plan, you are planning to fail—as the saying goes. Having a plan assumes you have clearly defined and written goals. If you work your plan on a daily basis you will create wealth as you achieve your goals. Included in your plan should be time for business, family, and spiritual—don't forget the spiritual part of the equation. It brings the whole into balance.

Make a Schedule

The second step is working a schedule. If you want to prosper, make a schedule and keep to it. Plan your day. You want to control events rather than have them control you. Have a fixed time each day for prospecting when you do not take phone calls, a time for appointments, and to going to real estate closings. You will create more wealth if you discipline yourself to follow this simple second step.

Prioritize Your Activity

The third step is prioritizing. Not all activity on your schedule is of the same importance. Do the most important things first and work down your list. If you have to find the funds to close a transaction, keep at it until you have it done. Tasks that have less importance can be relegated to an assistant. My assistant relives me of a great deal of work.

Work Only With Motivated Sellers and Qualified Buyers

The fourth step is spending time talking only to motivated sellers and qualifying your prospects. Talking to sellers who are not motivated is a waste of time. In the inflated equity of our local market, many people have put their houses up for sale just to see what will happen and hoping to get lucky. If a seller is not motivated the results can be discouraging and a waste or your time.

Don't waste the buyer's time either. You can easily determine if a buyer is serious or simply dreaming. They can dream on your time as long as you are secure knowing that you can help them achieve the dream, and you aren't investing too many hours on their dreams and too few on your own.

Education

The fifth step is taking time each day to further your education. Learn different techniques that will make you a better buyer, seller, negotiator, entrepreneur, closer, or keep you current with markets and trends. I spend the first hour of each morning increasing my real estate knowledge. At the gym each morning, you will find me reading a book on an investment-related subject while doing my cardio.

Attitude

The sixth step involves having the right kind of attitude. The fact is that bad things can happen during the day. The question becomes, will it control you or will you deal with the bad stuff and make something good out of it?

All of us face circumstances we did not plan. What helps make one person successful is how he or she handles the unexpected. I embrace the philosophy that says there is good in all situations—you just have to look for it. If a deal turns into a lemon, I try to make lemonade with it, sell it, and create wealth.

Plan to Give

The seventh step involves an idea that has been relegated to the rear of the philosophical bus. Most books and articles that tell us how to be successful are focused on "me." They are all about what *I* want, when *I* want it. I think that is dead wrong. If you want to truly enjoy success, you must first learn how to give away your wealth to others.

The principle of reciprocity is very real. The more you give, the more you get. I suggest that you learn to give away at least 10 percent of whatever you earn. If you cannot do that, your wealth owns you rather than you owning it. You can give to a charitable cause (you may even want to start one), educational foundations, mission projects—the list is endless—just give it with the thought of not receiving anything in return.

The result will be a satisfying, rich life. I give to others to enrich their lives. I not only share my wealth but also my time. Learn to give, and you'll be amazed at the results.

You can survive and even thrive in a slowing market. You just have to work smarter and plan for your success. Follow the seven steps and you will do just fine in any market. Now, it's your turn. Become a successful Real Estate Investor and share your success story with me. I'd love to hear it.

Glossary

A

Abstract

>A succinct summary; (for example, an abstract of judgment; an abstract of title, an abstract plant.)

Abstract of Judgment

>Summary of a court judgment creating a lien against a property when filed with the county recorder.

Abstract of Title

>The condensed history of a title to a particular parcel of real estate, consisting of a summary of the original grant and all subsequent conveyances and encumbrances affecting the property and a certification by the abstractor that the history is complete and accurate.

Abstract Plant

>A collection of information and documents relating to title of a particular property. Also known as "titleplant."

Acceleration Clause

>The clause in a mortgage or deed of trust that can be enforced to make the entire debt due immediately if the borrower defaults on an installment payment or other covenant.

Acceptance

>The written approval made by the seller from a buyer's offer.

Accrued
> On a closing statement, items of expense that are incurred but not yet payable, such as interest on a mortgage loan or taxes on real property.

Addendum
> Any addition or change to a contract.

Adjustable Rate Mortgage (ARM)
> A loan with an interest rate that fluctuates based on a specified financial index, such as Treasury securities or the 11th District Cost of Funds.

Agent
> A licensed representative of the state to conduct real estate transactions.

Agreement of Sale
> Also known as an agreement to convey. A signed, written contract entered into between the seller (vendor) and buyer (vendee) for sale of real property (land) under certain specific terms and conditions.

Alienation
> The transfer of property from one person to another. Alienation may be voluntary, such as by gift or sale, or involuntary, as through eminent domain or adverse possession.

Alienation Clause
A term of a mortgage requiring that the borrower
> pay in full the principal and interest due upon the sale of the property. (*See Acceleration or Due-on-Sale Clause*)

All-Inclusive Deed of Trust

A form of deed of trust that, in addition to any other amounts actually financed, includes the amounts of any prior deeds of trust. Sometimes referred to as a wrap-around or over-riding trust deed.

Amortization

Amortization is a schedule that outlines your loan payments for the duration of a loan. It details how much of each monthly payment goes toward the principal and how much goes toward paying off the loan balance. Initially, the bulk of your payments will be applied toward the interest. Many banks and title companies offer free amortization books. Be sure to ask for your copy. They're a handy tool.

Appraisal

Generally paid for by the buyer, the appraisal provides an estimate of a property's worth. Required by most lenders, it must be performed by a licensed appraiser before your home loan will be approved. The appraiser will arrive at a value based on the sale price of similar property. That is called "comparable" value.

Appraise

To fix or set a price or value upon.

Appreciation

The difference between the increased value of the property and the original value.

Arrears

Generally, being overdue in an installment payment.

Assessor

A municipality employee who estimates the value

of properties for the purpose of taxes.

Assignee

> The person to whom a transfer of interest is made. Hence, an assignee of an Agreement of Purchase and Sale may buy the property and enforce the contract in the same fashion as the original party.

Assignment

> The method by which a right or contract is transferred from one person (the assignor) to another (the assignee).

Assignor

> The person who makes an assignment to another person.

Assumable Mortgage

> A mortgage that can be taken over ("assumed") by the buyer when a home is sold. If interest rates have risen, an assumable mortgage at a low rate may prove a selling point for the property.

B

Balloon Payment

> A final payment of a mortgage loan that is considerably larger than the required periodic payments because the loan amount was not fully amortized.

Bankruptcy

An action filed in a federal bankruptcy court that
> allows a creditor to reorganize or discharge credit obligations due to insolvency. A property owner may halt foreclosure action by filing bankruptcy. Bankruptcies remain on a credit record for 7 years and can severely limit a person's ability to borrow.

- Chapter 7—"Debtor Wipeout." The court oversees the liquidation of the debtors' nonexempt assets, distributing the cash proceeds proportionally among creditors.

- Chapter 11—A Chapter 11 is a business reorganization proceeding.

- Chapter 13—"Debtor Workout." A Workout is the almost-automatic choice of most trustors seeking to use a bankruptcy filing to delay the inevitable trustee's sale as long as they can. The purpose of this proceeding is to give a wage earner time for rehabilitation . . . a temporary respite free from the collection efforts of creditors.

Beneficiary

A person entitled to receive money or assets from a trust or an estate. A lender is a beneficiary with a deed of trust or a note as a security for a loan.

Betterment

Any improvement of real estate that results in a rise in market value of that property.

Bid

An offer by an intending purchaser to pay a designated price for property that is about to be sold at auction.

Bill of Sale

Written document by which title to personal property (goods or chattels) is transferred from one party to another.

Blanket Deed of Trust
> A deed of trust secured by more than one lot or parcel of land.

Borrower
> The individual to whom a thing or money is lent at his request.

BPO
> Brokers Price Opinion.

Breach
> The breaking or violating of a law, a right, obligation, engagement, or duty, either by commission or omission.

Broker
> An agent authorized by the state to deal in real estate.

Brokerage
> The bringing together of two or more parties interested in making a real estate transaction.

Buy-Down mortgage
> A financing technique used to reduce the monthly payments for the first few years of a loan. Funds in the form of discount points are given to the lender by the builder or seller to buy down or lower the effective interest rate paid by the buyer, thus reducing the monthly payments for a set time.

Buyer's Broker (*Buyer's Agent, Buyer's Representative*)
> A Buyer Broker, as opposed to a Listing Broker, represents only the interests of the buyer. For a broker (also referred to as agent sometimes) to be considered a buyer's broker, an agreement must be made

between the buyer and the broker. Without such an agreement, the agent could end up representing the seller in a real estate transaction. In most states we now have what's call "Limited Dual Agency." Under this theory, a broker can represent both the buyer and the seller.

Buyers Market
A market condition where there are fewer buyers than there are sellers. Usually indicated when a property is on the market for more than 90 days and interest rates are very high. (12 percent or higher)

C

Capital Gain
A profit earned from the sale of an asset.

Cash Flow
The surplus after paying operating expenses and mortgage payments.

Certificate of Sale
A certificate issued at a judicial sale entitling the buyer to receive a deed after confirmation of court for the purchase of the property.

Chain of Title
A succession of conveyances comprising the title record history to a specific parcel of real property. Chattel Personal property, such as household items.

Chattel Mortgage
A mortgage secured by personal property.

Closing Costs
This is the final step in the home buying/selling

process. The loan documents are signed and finalized at this point. After the documents are signed, notarized, and the money submitted to satisfy all the debts, the transfer of the deed is made from the buyer to the seller when the title company (or attorney) files the deed and any supporting documentation with the country clerk. The filing of the documents with the county clerk signifies closing has occurred.

Closing Date

The agreed-upon date for a buyer to take over property.

Cloud on Title

Any outstanding claim that contradicts the title record, and if valid, would impair the owner's title.

Code

A collection of laws relating to a certain topic, such as real property or patents.

Cosigner

A cosigner signs a promissory note and takes responsibility for the debt.

Collateral

Real estate or personal property pledged as security for a debt.

Collection

Obtaining payment or the liquidation of a debt or claim, either by personal solicitation or legal proceedings.

Comparables

Similar properties used as yardsticks to determine

the market value of a certain property.

Complaint
> The original or initial pleading by which an action is commenced; a written statement of the essential facts constituting the offense charged.

Condemnation
> A judicial or administrative proceeding to exercise the power of eminent domain, through which a government agency takes private property for public use and compensates the owner.

Contingency
> A specified condition that must be fulfilled before a contract becomes firm and binding.

Contract
> An agreement between two or more persons creating an obligation to do or not to do a particular thing.

Conventional Loan
> A loan that requires no insurance or guarantees.

Conveyance
> A written instrument that transfers title to or an interest in land from one party to another (for example, a deed, an assignment, or a bill of sale)

Counteroffer
> A response given to an offer.

Credit report
> A document from a credit bureau setting forth a credit rating and pertinent financial data concerning a person or a company and used by banks, merchants, suppliers and the like in evaluating a

credit risk.

Creditor

One to whom money is owed.

D

Debt

A sum of money due by a certain and express agreement; a specified sum of money owing to one person from another, including not only obligation of debtor to pay but the right of the creditor to receive and enforce payment.

Debt Ratio

To compare the total monthly payments of all of the borrower's debts (including the mortgage) with the gross monthly income of the borrower. It evaluates the borrower's ability to pay mortgage. Also referred to as Debt-to-Income ratio.

Debtor

An entity that owes a debt; one who owes a debt.

Decree of Foreclosure

A court order to set out the outstanding amount on a delinquent mortgage in order to sell the property to pay the mortgagee.

Deed

A written instrument that, when executed and delivered, conveys title to or an interest in real estate.

Deed in Lieu of Foreclosure

A process whereby the owner, with the approval of the lender, deeds the property to the lender to avoid foreclosure. Lenders are generally reluctant to accept a deed in lieu unless the title is free and clear of any other encumbrances junior to theirs and the owners execute an estoppel affidavit acknowledging that they are acting volitionally, with informed consent.

Deed of Reconveyance

An instrument that releases and discharges a deed of trust, when the mortgage has been paid out.

Deed of Trust (Trust Deed)

A three party security instrument conveying the legal title to real property as security for the repayment of a loan. The owner is called the trustor. The neutral third party to whom the bare legal title is conveyed (and who is called on to liquidate the property if need be) is the trustee. The lender is the beneficiary. When the loan is paid off, the trustee is directed by the beneficiary to issue a deed of reconveyance to the trustor, which extinguishes the trust deed lien.

Default

The failure to make payments in full on time or at all or to live up to any other obligations placed on the borrower by the loan agreement.

Defeasance Clause

A clause used in leases and mortgages that cancels a specified right upon the occurrence of a certain condition, such as cancellation of a mortgage upon repayment of the mortgage loan.

Defendant

The person who defends against a claim asserted in a court action.

Deficiency Judgment

A judgment entered in a lawsuit when a property is sold for less than the amount of the loan.

Delinquency
> A condition when the payment is late but not yet in default.

Demand Letter
> Also known as a Breach Letter or Notice of Intent to Foreclose. Notice to the borrower that he/she is in "breach" of the terms of the Note and advising of the right to cure the default.

Department of Housing and Urban Development (HUD)
> A federal agency focusing on programs regarding housing and renewal of city communities.

Department of Veterans Affairs (VA)
> An independent federal agency overseeing programs for military veterans, including loan and mortgage programs. This agency allows most veterans to purchase a house without a down payment.

Disclosure Statement
> Document disclosing the terms of a loan.

Due-on-Sale Clause
> A clause in a mortgage that requires that the mortgage be paid out in full upon the sale of the property.

Due Diligence
> Such a measure of prudence, activity, or assiduity as is properly to be expected from a reasonable and prudent man under the particular circumstance.

E

Earnest Money Deposit

> Along with an offer, buyers can make a deposit on the home to demonstrate the seriousness of the offer. When an earnest money deposit is made, it is held by an escrow until closing. It is then added to the down payment.

Easement

> A right of way allowing someone to cross over another's property for certain purposes, such as power lines or water mains.

Encroachment

> A fixture that illegally intrudes into or invades the property or encloses a portion of it, diminishing its width or area.

Encumbrance

> Anything, such as a mortgage, tax, or judgment lien, an easement, or restriction on the use of the land or an outstanding dower right that may diminish the value or use and enjoyment of a property.

Equity

> The surplus of value that may remain after existing liens are deducted from the property.

Equity Right of Redemption

> The right to avoid foreclosure action by paying off the debts, interest, and fees that accumulated on the property.

Escrow Account

> Funds held before closing by a third party, usually including the earnest money deposit. Future taxes and homeowners insurance, held by the mortgage

company after closing, are also considered escrow.

Estate
> The total assets a person has when he dies, including real property.

Estoppel Certificate
> A certificate in which a borrower certifies the amount owed on a mortgage loan and the rate of interest.

Eviction
> The act of depriving a person of the possession of land or rental property held or leased.

F

Fair Market Value
> The amount at which property would change hands between a willing buyer and a willing seller, neither being under any compulsion to buy or sell and both having reasonable knowledge of the relevant facts.

Fannie Mae
> It's an official name of the Federal National Mortgage Association, which is one of the largest agencies that buys mortgages from lenders and resells them as securities on the secondary mortgage market.

FHA – Federal Housing Administration
> FHA is a branch of the Department of Housing and Urban Development (HUD). The agency's basic function is to direct housing in a way that Congress mandates by issuing mortgage insurance to institutional lenders on the loans they make. With such loan insurance, lenders are willing to lend with smaller down payments and at lower rates of interest.

FHA Loans

A loan program offering low-rate mortgages to buyers willing to make a down payment as little as 3 percent.

First Mortgage

A mortgage that is in first position and has priority as a lien over all other mortgages.

FSBO – For Sale By Owner

This term refers to property being sold without a real estate broker. FSBO is also used to refer to the homeowner who is selling the property.

Foreclosure

A legal procedure whereby property used as security for a debt is sold to satisfy the debt in the event of default in payment of the mortgage note or default of other terms in the mortgage document. The foreclosure procedure brings the rights of all parties to a conclusion and passes the title in the mortgaged property to either the holder of the mortgage or a third party who may purchase the realty at the foreclosure sale, free of all encumbrances affecting the property subsequent to the mortgage.

G

Garnishment

A statutory proceeding whereby a person's property, money, credits in possession or under the control of, or owing by, another are applied to payment of the former's debt to third person by proper statutory process against debtor and garnishee.

Good Faith Estimate

Institutional lender estimates the costs a borrower will incur, including inspection fees and loanprocessing charges.

Grace Period
> A period of days during which a debtor may cure a delinquency without penalty (before triggering a late charge, a foreclosure, or an acceleration of the balance due).

Grantee
> The person to whom the title of the property is granted.

Grantor
> The person (seller) who grants title to another person (buyer).

H
Habendum Clause
> Meaning "to have and to hold," which defines the quantity of the estate transferred to the new owner of land.

Home Equity Line of Credit
> Sometimes referred to as an HELOC, a Home Equity Line of Credit is a loan that a property owner secures that can be repaid and borrowed again at the owner's convenience.

Home Equity Loan
> Borrowing against the equity in one's home.

HUD 1 Statement
> A form, usually given by a bank, that includes the costs of purchasing a home.

Hypothecate
> When you use something as security and still retain

possession of it.

I

Indemnify
> Any losses and damages an individual endures for which you are fully responsible.

Instrument
> A legal written document.

Involuntary lien
> A lien issued against a property without an owner's approval.

J

Joint Ownership
> When two or more parties own the same property.

Joint Venture
> A project where two or more individuals take part in a business transaction to share the cost, risk, and reward.

Judgment
> The final decision of the court resolving a dispute and determining the rights and obligations of the parties.

Judicial Foreclosure
> A foreclosure process executed through a court action.

Junior lien
> A lien that is subordinate or junior to a senior lien.

L

Land Contract

An agreement used to sell real property that transfers ownership of the property, but the title does not transfer until most or the entire purchase price is paid.

Landlord

He who, being the owner of an estate of land, or rental property, leased it to another.

Lease

An agreement involving payment of rent for possession of real estate for a specific period of time.

Lease Option

A lease that contains the right to purchase a property for a specific price during a given time frame.

Lender

He from whom a thing or money is borrowed.

Lien

A claim or charge on a property for payment of some debt, obligation or duty.

Life Estate

An estate whose duration is limited to the life of the party holding it.

Lis pendens

A term meaning "legal action pending," giving notice of an action or proceeding affecting the title of the property.

Loss Mitigation Department

A department that helps homeowners avoid

foreclosure; the lender tries to help a borrower who has been unable to make loan payments and in danger of defaulting on a loan

Lot Book Report
A title record report given by a title company announcing encumbrances recorded against the property.

M
Marketable Title
A title with no claims or defects that could otherwise hinder a property being sold.

Mechanic's lien
A claim created by state statutes for the purpose of securing priority of payment of the price or value of work performed and materials furnished in erecting or repairing a building or other structure, and as such, attaches to the land as well as buildings and improvements erected thereon.

Mortgage
An interest in land created by a written instrument providing security for the performance of a duty or the payment of a debt.

Mortgagee
The entity, usually a bank or financial institution that lends money to a borrower.

Mortgagor
The person borrowing money from a lender to purchase a property.

Multiple Listings Service (MLS)
A listing of properties from local real estate agents

that consist of homes available in an area. For-Sale by-Owner properties are not listed in this database.

N

NARCA

> National Association of Retail Collection Attorneys

Notice of Default (NOD)

> A notice sent by a lender when a mortgage payment is late in an attempt to cure or make the loan current.

Notice of Rescission

> A legal document used when the defaulting party either cured or corrected a default.

Notice of Sale

> The notice of an impending foreclosure sale the state requires. The notice recites the legal description of the property being foreclosed upon and gives the time, date, and place of the pending sale.

O

Offer to Purchase

> A contract expressing a person's willingness to purchase a certain property on terms expressed in the offer.

Owner Financing (Seller Financing)

> A creative method in real estate where the seller of a property agrees to finance all or some of the property. In a sense, the owner acts as a bank.

P

Power of Attorney

> A written document signed by the owner that authorizes someone else to act in behalf of the

owner.

Power of Sale

A clause commonly inserted in mortgages and deeds of trust that are in default, giving the mortgagee (or trustee) the right and power to advertise and sell the mortgaged property at public auction to satisfy the debt.

Pre-Foreclosure

Term used to discuss delinquent properties before they go to the foreclosure auction.

Q
Quit Title

An action to remove an adverse claim or cloud from the title of property.

Quit Claim Deed

A deed of conveyance that releases any title, interest, or claim the grantor may have in the premises.

R
Real Estate Owned (REO)

Property acquired by the lender after it went to auction.

Recorder

A public official responsible for keeping the records of real estate transactions.

Redemption Period

The time allotted to the mortgagor to reclaim property after being sold at an auction. Not all states have a redemption period.

S

Sales Contract
>A contract to which the buyer and seller agree to terms of sale.

Second Mortgage
>A second loan placed upon a property in addition to an existing first loan.

Seller Financing
>A creative method in real estate where the seller of a property agrees to finance all or some of the property. In a sense, the owner acts like a bank.

Sellers Market
>When the market conditions are such that the sellers have the advantage and multiple offers are made.

Sheriff's Sale
>The sale of a property to satisfy a debt or judgment.

Short Sale
>The sale of a property under or at market value lower than the loan balance.

Simultaneous Closing
>The term "simultaneous closing" refers to two closings occurring at the same time. This is a creative technique used when traditional financing will not work.

Subject To
>The transfer of rights to pay a debt from one party to another, with the original party remaining liable for the debt if the second party defaults.

Survey
>The process by which a parcel of land is measured

and its boundaries and contents set forth.

Tax Deed
> A type of deed used to convey title after real property is sold at auction by public authority for nonpayment of taxes.

Tax Lien
> A lien on real estate in favor of a state or local government that may be foreclosed on for the nonpayment of taxes.

Tenant
> A person in possession of real property with the owner's permission.

Tenant at Sufferance
> A person who after rightfully being in possession of a rented premises continues to live in that premises after his right has terminated.

Tenant at Will
> One who holds possession of premises with the owner's permission.

Title
> Evidence of ownership of land.

Title Company
> Firms that examine properties to ensure that the title to a piece of property is clear and free of any encumbrances. They also issue title insurance.

Title Insurance
> An insurance policy that provides protection for lenders and buyers against any losses caused by defects in the title.

Title Report
> A report which sets out the current state of title to a property.

Title Search
> A search within the public records to determine ownership and that there are no claims or liens against the property.

Torrens Title
> A Torrens Title contains a listing of all legal instruments (mortgages, judgments, liens) that have been recorded on the property from its origin.

Trust Account
> A special account used by a broker or escrow agent to safeguard funds for a buyer or seller.

Trust Deed
> A three party security instrument conveying the legal title to real property as security for the repayment of a loan. The owner is called the trustor. The neutral third party to whom the bare legal title is conveyed (and who is called on to liquidate the property if need be) is the trustee. The lender is the beneficiary. When the loan is paid off, the trustee is directed by the beneficiary to issue a deed of reconveyance to the trustor, which extinguishes the trust deed lien.

Trustee
> A legally empowered person who holds or controls a piece of property for another person.

Trustee's Deed
> A deed given to the successful high bidder after a

foreclosure auction.

Trustee's Sale
> An auction where a trustee may sell a property that has defaulted in effort to pay the outstanding debt that is owed.

U
UCC
> Uniform Commercial Code; uniform laws drafted by the National Conference of Commissioners on Uniform State Laws governing commercial transactions.

Undivided Interest
> Ownership of real estate by joint tenants under the same title.

Unsecured Debt
> Debt not secured by collateral.

Upset Price
> The opening bid amount that begins the auction bidding during a foreclosure sale.

V
VA Loans
> A program that allows the purchase of a house without a down payment to most veterans.

Vacate
> To make vacant or empty.

W
Warranty Deed
> Deed in which the grantor warrants good clear title.

Without Recourse
> Giving the lender no right to seek payment or seize assets in the event of nonpayment from anyone other than the party specified in the debt contract.

Wraparound Mortgage
> The financing technique in which payment of the existing mortgage is continued by the seller and a new, higher interest loan (larger than the existing mortgage) is paid by the borrower.

Y
Yield
> The return on investment or the amount of profit stated as a percentage of the amount invested.

Z
Zoning
> Regulations that control the use of land within a jurisdiction.

www.ingramcontent.com/pod-product-compliance
Lightning Source LLC
Chambersburg PA
CBHW061158180526
45170CB00002B/854